31 *Yangchuanosaurus*
32 *Psittacosaurus*
33 *Barapasaurus*
34 *Kentrosaurus*
35 *Giraffatitan*
36 *Nqwebasaurus*
37 *Heterodontosaurus*
38 allosaur
39 *Massospondylus*
40 hypsilophodontid
41 polacanthid
42 camarasaurid
43 *Cryolophosaurus*
44 *Massospondylus*

In memory of Rudy Zallinger, dino-artist and inspiration to generations of young paleontologists. Your mural *The Age of Reptiles* got me into science when I was in the fourth grade, and it's been a wonderful life ever since.
—R.T.B.

For my lifelong companion, Carmen Naranjo, and my kids from Metepec, Mexico, for permanent inspiration, love . . . and everything. I'd also like to specially thank Flo and Charlie Magovern, David Hone, the SVPCA and SVP gangs, and Christopher Ries for their priceless, continuous support.
—L.V.R.

Text copyright © 2013 by Dr. Robert T. Bakker
Cover and interior illustrations copyright © 2013 by Luis V. Rey

Visit us on the Web!
randomhouse.com/kids

Educators and librarians, for a variety of teaching tools, visit us at RHTeachersLibrarians.com

Library of Congress Cataloging-in-Publication Data
Bakker, Robert T., author.
The big golden book of dinosaurs / by Dr. Robert T. Bakker ; illustrated by Luis V. Rey. — First edition.
    p. cm.
Includes index.
ISBN 978-0-375-85958-8 (trade) — ISBN 978-0-375-96679-8 (lib. bdg.)
1. Dinosaurs—Juvenile literature. I. Rey, Luis V., ill. II. Title.
QE861.5.B3435 2013   567.9—dc23   2012020147
MANUFACTURED IN MALAYSIA

10 9 8 7 6 5 4 3 2 1

The Big Golden Book of
DINOSAURS

BY DR. ROBERT T. BAKKER

ILLUSTRATED BY LUIS V. REY

Apatosaurus

A GOLDEN BOOK · NEW YORK

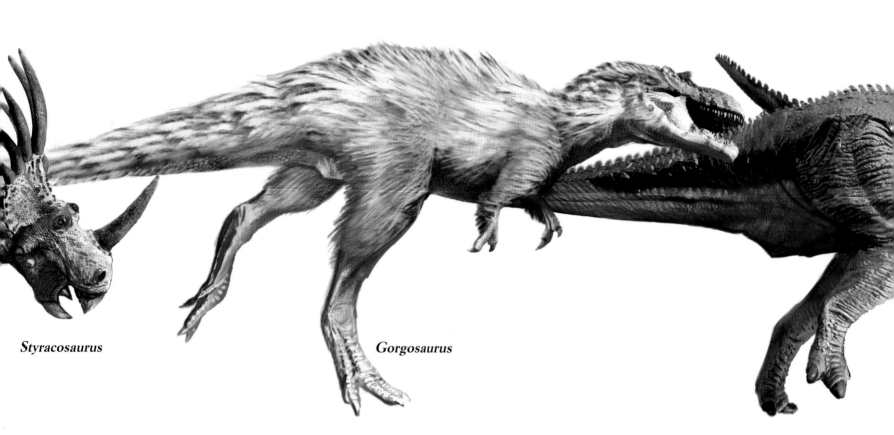

Styracosaurus   *Gorgosaurus*

CONTENTS

Maiasaura

Lambeosaurus

Tyrannosaurus

Edmontosaurus

Pentaceratops

DINOSAURS

No other prehistoric creatures are so exciting—or mysterious. Some dinosaurs were heavier than two dozen elephants duct-taped together. Others were as tiny as kittens. Some had jaws so strong they could bite through a school bus. There were even dinosaurs who could fly.

Dinosaurs ruled the earth for over 150 million years. Their heads and bodies evolved—changed through time—in a thousand different ways. How do we know? From fossils. Fossils are the remains left by plants or animals, preserved in layers of stone. Dinosaur bones and teeth and poop and footprints became fossilized when they were buried in soft sand and clay. Then minerals, dissolved in water, worked like glue to harden the sediment and turned it into rock.

But the dinosaurs didn't live alone. Fossils show us that they lived with bugs and frogs and many other kinds of animals. Dinosaurs were just one part of a great family tree of animals with backbones. One branch of this tree evolved into amphibians with soft skin, like frogs. Meanwhile, another branch was evolving into scaly lizards and turtles, alligators and crocodiles, and dinosaurs. And at the same time the third branch was evolving into furry mammals.

That's right. Our own distant ancestors lived with the dinosaurs, and dinosaurs hunted them. So the dinosaur story is our story, too.

Ankylosaurus

Oviraptor

Brachiosaurus

9

THE DEVONIAN PERIOD: ARMOR-PLATED DINO FISH AND THE CONQUEST OF LAND

Are dinosaur skeletons the oldest fossil bones from prehistoric monsters? No. Not even close.

The oldest giant skeletons come from the Devonian Period, 370 million years ago. That's long, long before there were any dinosaurs.

Imagine that we're in the shallow, warm ocean covering what is now Cleveland. Look! A graceful shark leaps out of the waves. Something big and fast is chasing it from below.

It's the Gorgon Fish—*Gorgonichthys*—and it's as big as a killer whale. The Gorgon Fish has bone armor all over its head and back. There's a special joint at its shoulders so that when the Gorgon bites, its entire head snaps down like a bear trap.

Up a nearby river are two other Devonian creatures. They're superstars of evolution, relatives of dinosaurs . . . and of us! Lurking near the surface is *Panderichthys,* the Lizard Fish.

Gorgonichthys

acanthodians

Watch carefully—it can do some very unfishy things. Like poke its snout out of the water and inhale. Lizard Fish have both gills and lungs so they can breathe underwater and in the air!

Panderichthys's fins are even more astounding. The fin bones are covered with muscles that bulge out in lobes. That's why it's also called a lobe fin. *Panderichthys* uses its muscular fins to push through dense weeds.

And there's *Acanthostega,* "Spiny Armor." It's ugly, with a wide, flat head like an alligator and a tail like a fish. And instead of fins, it has stubby legs with short toes. *Acanthostega* is one of the very first animals that can walk on four feet. It evolved over millions of years from a lobe-fin fish relative of *Panderichthys*.

Acanthostega is an amphibian, a creature that lays eggs in the water or on moist ground the way frogs do now. Look carefully at its toes. Most four-footed critters alive today have no more than five toes. *Acanthostega* has eight. Those extra toes will get trimmed off as its descendants evolve.

All four-footed creatures evolved from an ancestor like *Acanthostega*—including dinosaurs and possums and chimpanzees and humans.

Panderichthys

Acanthostega

THE PERMIAN AND CARBONIFEROUS PERIODS: MONSTER BUGS, FROGOIDS, AND FEROCIOUS FIN-BACKS

Let's travel to the Late Carboniferous Period, about 320 million years ago. We're in a hot, humid forest near Scotland. Flowers haven't yet evolved. All the trees and bushes are dull green and look like ferns or pine trees or horsetail plants. There are swamps fifty miles wide, filled to the brim with rotting vegetation. When all this compost gets buried under layers of sand, it will change into coal.

New amphibians large and small thrive in the warm water. They lay eggs in water or moist soil and their babies breathe through gills.

Who rules the dry land? Big bugs! The mammoth millipede *Arthropleura* is so wide you could hop on its back and ride it. *Arthropleura* is a plant-eater. But there are giant meat-eating bugs, too—super-scorpions two and a half feet long. *Bzzz. BZZZZZ.* Something swoops down from the sky. It's a dragonfly more than two feet wide. Why are Carboniferous bugs so immense? Today, the lungs of scorpions, dragonflies, and millipedes don't work well if the animal gets too big. But extra oxygen in the Coal Age air might have let bugs get super-sized.

The giant dragonfly grabs a squirmy critter about eleven inches long. She's a *Hylonomus* and she fights back, kicking wildly. Amphibians have soft toe tips, but *Hylonomus* has hard, sharp-tipped claws. She scratches the dragonfly's face. *Ouch!* The dragonfly drops his would-be prey.

Hylonomus digs into the leaf litter, hollowing out a hole as big as a coffee cup. Then she does something amazing. She lays hard-shelled eggs and buries them. Warmed by the sun, the eggs mature. Six weeks later, they hatch. The babies don't have gills and they don't swim in the water. Instead, they breathe air and start hunting prey on land right away. *Hylonomus* is not an amphibian—she's a reptile. Her kin will become the ancestors of all turtles and lizards and snakes, all gators and crocodiles, and all dinosaurs. Plus some of her kin will evolve into mammals.

Meganeura

Hylonomus

anthracosaur

As the Carboniferous ended and the Permian began, the big swamps dried up. Now the landscape is dotted with small ponds and dry meadows. During the summer droughts, amphibians crowd into the few remaining pools. Here we find hundreds of *Diplocaulus*, aka Boomerang Head, one of the weirdest amphibians of all time. *Diplocaulus* swing their banana-shaped skulls sideways, clunking each other as hard as they can. *Thud. Thud.* Head clunking is their way of fighting for the best position on the pond bottom—the place where the most worms and small fish can be found.

Diplocaulus

Boomerang Heads spend their whole lives in water, using gills to breathe. The armadillo toad, *Platyhystrix,* lives a double life. It hatches in ponds, then leaves the water to hunt on dry land. *Platyhystrix* has a thick fin on its back that makes it look taller and more dangerous. That's especially useful in the mating season, when the animals try to impress each other. Many other Permian animals evolved tall fins, too.

Eryops

Platyhystrix

What happened to those small reptiles of the Carboniferous, like *Hylonomus* and its relatives? Some have evolved into magnificent beasts. *Edaphosaurus,* the fin-back "Ship Lizard," is as heavy as a pony and one of the first big four-footed animals on land to eat plants. Ship Lizards chop up leaves and branches with hundreds of sharp little teeth. Other early reptiles have evolved into the first big reptilian predators. *Dimetrodon* is a sixteen-foot-long fin-back killer as heavy as a tiger.

When most people see a *Dimetrodon* in a museum, they think it's a dinosaur.

Dimetrodon

Edaphosaurus

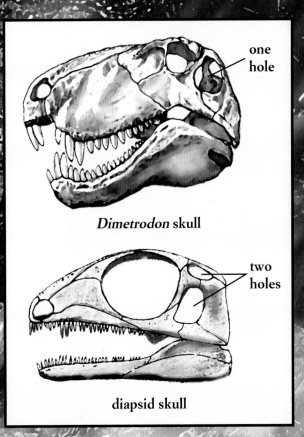

one
hole

Dimetrodon skull

two
holes

diapsid skull

But it's not. You
can tell by looking
at the back of its skull.
There's a single hole
behind the eye. That hole
is special—the jaw muscles
are attached all along its
edge. No dinosaur had that
single hole—and so *Dimetrodon*
is not a dinosaur. *Edaphosaurus* is a
one-holer, too.

Many other famous animals also have that one-
hole design. Humans have it. So do dogs and cats and
horses and elephants. All warm-blooded mammals are one-
holers, descended from a *Dimetrodon*-like ancestor. So put a
picture of *Dimetrodon* next to Grandma and Grandpa in your living
room—the fin-back is in your family tree!

If we look carefully, we might see a small, long-legged reptile zipping
across the Permian mudflats and running up tree trunks, chasing roaches. It's a
diapsid—a two-holer. Look behind its eye—there are two holes on each side. Who
has a two-hole skull? Lizards and snakes and crocodiles and alligators—and dinosaurs.

diapsid

THE LATE TRIASSIC PERIOD: RULING REPTILES AND FLEET-FOOTED DINOSAURS

We're in the Petrified Forest region of what is now Arizona. It's the Late Triassic, 215 million years ago. The climate is still dry, as it was in the Permian, but the trees look more modern. There are conifers with needles like today's monkey puzzle tree, and cycadeoid trees with huge palm-shaped leaves. Flowering plants still haven't evolved.

Crouching on the bottom of a lazy river is one of the last big amphibians—a metoposaur. It looks like a short-legged alligator that was flattened by a steamroller. It's a patient predator. It just sits on the muddy bottom, waiting to ambush something.

On dry land, *Dimetrodon* and his kin are extinct, along with most of the other one-hole reptiles that ruled the Permian. But new kinds of reptiles have evolved. Up in a tree a dozen tiny flying lizards squabble over a fat, juicy roach. One lizard falls . . . then *flip!* Wings made of skin—stretched tight by special ribs—open wide and the lizard floats gently to the ground. If you had X-ray vision, you'd see two holes behind the eye in the flying lizard's skull, so you'd know that it evolved from that little diapsid reptile we saw in the Permian.

ZOOM! A bat-winged *Eudimorphodon* just misses the little lizard. *Eudimorphodon* is a dactyl, another clan of Triassic fliers. It flaps its strong wings and zips back up into the sky.

The top Triassic predators are new, too. *Poposaurus* is eighteen feet long, with saw-edged fangs like those of *Dimetrodon*. But *Poposaurus* is much taller and faster. A narrow row of bone armor protects his back. The top plant-eater is *Desmatosuchus*. She has wide bone armor plates on her back, throat, and belly. On her shoulders are great curved horns. She swings her forequarters and tries to skewer the poposaur. He dances around trying to find a soft spot to bite. Impossible!

metoposaur

Eudimorphodon

Poposaurus

Desmatosuchus

Poposaurus and *Desmatosuchus* are so big and scary-looking that we might suspect that they are dinosaurs. But they're not quite. They're close relatives of dinosaurs. Whenever we want to unlock the mysteries of who is related to whom, we go back to the skull holes. Poposaurs and desmatosuchs have two openings behind the eye, so they are descendants of a diapsid reptile. But there's an extra hole in their snout, between the nostril and eyeball. That makes them three-holers. The three-hole clan has a special label: Archosauria, which means "Ruling Reptiles." Archosaurs filled the Triassic with new and wonderful groups, including crocodiles and dactyls.

The first dinosaurs show up in the Triassic, too. Are they archosaurs? Yes! Their skulls are three-holers. But dinosaurs added special joints in the neck and feet that make them the fastest and most graceful archosaurs. Here's a fine example of the dino-body plan—

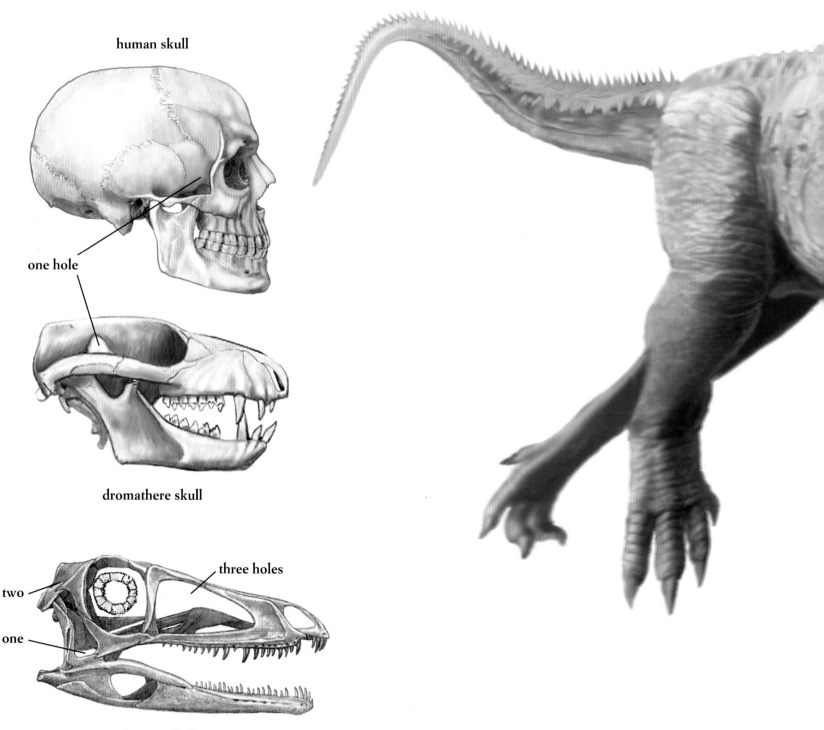

human skull

one hole

dromathere skull

two

three holes

one

archosaur skull

Chindesaurus. He's five feet long and about as heavy as a Labrador retriever. Most Triassic land animals ran flat-footed. Not chindesaurs. They kept their ankles high off the ground like ballet dancers. And chindesaurs had slender necks bent into S-shaped curves, so they could reach out and grab prey. All the later dinosaurs—including *T. rex*—came from ancestors like *Chindesaurus.*

There's one more Late Triassic creature you should meet. It's *Dromatherium,* a mouse-sized predator that crunches bugs with its prickly molar teeth. Dromatheres and their kind are not close relatives of dinosaurs. They're one-holers. They're evolving extraordinary new things: glands on their chests so the mothers can supply milk to their babies, and hair. Dromatheres are almost mammals.

Chindesaurus

Dromatherium

THE LATE JURASSIC PERIOD: HUNDRED-FOOT-LONG DINOSAURS AND SPIKE-TAILS

As the Triassic ended and the Jurassic Period began, the world was shaken by mass extinctions. The fierce poposaurs and plant-eating desmatosuchians died out. Who would evolve to fill the empty spots? New clans of dinosaurs! Some would grow to stupendous sizes.

Apatosaurus

Brachiosaurus

Camarasaurus

Allosaurus

Imagine that it is 145 million years ago in southern Wyoming. The forests still don't have any flowers. Tall conifers with needles like pine trees' grow near streams and ponds. The Wyoming dry seasons are so severe that giant herbivorous dinosaurs have to migrate hundreds of miles to find green leaves. When the first big dark rain clouds appear in the sky, it's the signal for the dino herds to come back to the Wyoming meadows.

As the rainy season begins, we see a dust cloud rise a thousand feet. It's not the wind swirling the dust. Hundreds of dinosaur paws, four feet wide, are churning up the dry soil. *SNAP!* The dinosaurs fight by snapping their whiplike tails.

Amphicoelias

Dryosaurus

It's a great herd of *Amphicoelias,* long-necked plant-eaters that can grow to be over a hundred feet long. Their neck bones are hollow and full of air. This makes them so light that they can be swung sideways very fast. *THUD.* The dinosaurs are hitting each other giraffe-style.

Allosaurus

Camarasaurus

Baby *Amphicoelias* hurry across a dry sandbar to catch up with
their moms. The hungry herbivores sniff around at ground level, but
all the plants are dry and brown. One big bull straightens up and sniffs—
he senses fresh leaves far above in the treetops. Too far to reach unless . . .
He balances on his hind legs and uses his tail to prop up his body. He tilts his body up,
up, up . . . until his nose touches the top of the trees. He doesn't chew. He simply chops
off branches and swallows. Gizzard stones in his stomach will grind the food.

Allosaurus, a two-ton meat-eater, slowly stalks across a meadow following a scent trail.
He's met by an angry five-ton plant-eater, a *Stegosaurus. Swoosh!* She swings her spike-
studded tail.

Swoosh . . . whack! The stegosaur scores a direct hit. One spike goes straight up into the
allosaur's lower hip bone. For a second, it doesn't hurt. Then the throbbing begins.

Apatosaurus

Stegosaurus

The allosaur retreats to his lair along the riverbank. In the next few weeks, infection spreads. Finally, the allosaur dies. His body is buried when the river overflows and spreads a blanket of goopy mud over the lair. In 1997, his skeleton will be dug up by my crew from the Paleon Museum of Glenrock, Wyoming.

Brachiosaurus

Apatosaurus

Our mammal relatives have multiplied since the Triassic. Furry mammals come in a dozen different clans, all small. Most probably laid eggs like the modern-day duckbill platypus. Which furball is closest to human ancestry? *Foxraptor!* It's only half the size of a house mouse, but it has evolved the most advanced teeth—molars with five cusps each. When it chews beetles, the cusps interlock and chop bug parts with great efficiency. Humans have five-cusp molars, too, though the cusp points are blunt, better for chewing vegetables.

Ornitholestes

Foxraptor

MONSTERS OF THE JURASSIC SEAS AND THE TWELVE-YEAR-OLD GIRL WHO DISCOVERED THEM

The Jurassic seas were full of reptilian monsters who were not dinosaurs, and we'll meet them now. We'll also meet the first person who was paid to dig Jurassic skeletons and get them into museums—twelve-year-old Mary Anning, of Lyme Regis, England.

In 1800, Mary Anning was a year old and sitting up in her baby carriage. *Bzaam!* It was hit by lightning. From that day on, neighbors said she was a most unusual child. When she was eight years old, she began helping her parents sell Jurassic seashells from their shop at the seashore. They couldn't afford to send Mary to school, but friends lent her science books and she devoured them. Then in 1811, Mary excavated a Jurassic skeleton that made her famous. It was an ocean-going reptile with a combination of body parts never seen before. The skull was lizard-like, but the teeth were like a crocodile's. The legs were flippers. And the tail and torso were like a fast-swimming shark's. Museum scientists named the reptile *Ichthyosaurus,* or "Fish Lizard."

Mary dug more ichthyosaurs. Some had fish scales still inside the guts, proof that ichthyosaurs were fish-eaters. Inspired by Mary's discovery, German fossil hunters began digging for ichthyosaurs. Inside one skeleton were seven tiny Fish Lizard skeletons—unborn babies. One was found halfway through the birth canal. These fossils proved that Fish Lizards didn't come on land to lay eggs, the way modern sea turtles do. Instead, the babies were born at sea, like porpoises.

A few years later, Mary discovered another clan of sea reptile. Its neck was long and slender, and its head had dozens of sharp teeth that interlocked when the jaws closed. Both its front and back legs were long flippers of the sort that sea lions and penguins have today.

Professors of geology were flabbergasted. Jurassic seas were full of unexpected monsters. They named the long-necked reptile *Plesiosaurus.* Sea lions and penguins can dive and do backflips—and they have only one pair of flippers. Plesiosaurs had *two* pairs and must have been even better at maneuvers.

Inside Mary's plesiosaur were hundreds of little hooks from the suckers of squid, direct evidence of what sort of seafood these reptiles preferred.

Both ichthyosaurs and plesiosaurs had two holes behind the eye, so we know they evolved from a diapsid reptile of the Permian Period.

Dimorphodon

Ichthyosaurus

Dimorphodon

Ichthyosaurus

Mary's third famous find was the first dactyl ever dug in England, *Dimorphodon*. A few years later, German fossil diggers uncovered more Jurassic dactyl skeletons that preserved the wing surface. Dactyl wings were made of tough skin, stretched between the super-strong arms and the back legs, like bat wings today. So dactyls must have been the fighter-bombers of their day, fast and maneuverable. Mary's *Dimorphodon* could swoop down and snatch fish and squid swimming near the surface.

Back in the early 1800s, young women were supposed to be quiet. But Mary corrected professors when they got their bones wrong. A few fussy German scholars complained that she was "uppity," but scientists from Oxford University found her charming. They were so impressed, they paid for her portrait to be painted and hung in the office of the Geological Society. She was the first woman scientist to be so honored.

Plesiosaurus

squid

FLUFFY DINOSAURS

During the Jurassic, dinosaurs were evolving in every sort of direction. Some became huge. Some got armor. Others developed long shins and ankles that let them run super-fast. And some meat-eaters were becoming fluffy. Yes, fluffy! How scientists discovered dino-fluffiness is a fantastic story.

In the early 1800s, scientists thought that dinosaurs had big, flat feet and skin covered with scales. They were wrong. Here's how the mistake happened: The first skeleton discovered of a meat-eating dinosaur was a *Megalosaurus*—a creature about as heavy as a rhino. Before the megalosaur was buried, its body had been pulled apart by scavengers that yanked the leg bones out of position. The bone jumble confused the scientists. They found huge bones that looked sort of like the shoulder of a lizard. Since lizards are flat-footed and have five toes, the megalosaur was reconstructed as a five-toed flat-foot. The poor dinosaur looked awkward and slow.

megalosaur wrong

giant shoulder?

The megalosaur jaw looked like a croc's, and its saw-edged teeth looked like a lizard's. And that's why scientists made sculptures of the megalosaur with scaly skin like a croc's or a lizard's.

Whenever another meat-eating dinosaur was dug up, it was restored the same way, with flat-footed, five-toed paws in front and behind. Meanwhile, fossil footprints were being discovered in Jurassic and Cretaceous rocks, and although bones from flat-footed megalosaurs seemed to be everywhere, no one could find a single megalosaur footprint. Weird!

The mystery would begin to be solved in the 1830s by the Reverend Edward Hitchcock of Massachusetts. Hitchcock dug thousands of Jurassic footprints from mysterious animals. Because of their sharp claws, Hitchcock concluded that the creatures were predators. But what kind? Hitchcock's mystery track-makers were not flat-footed, so he figured the footprints were not from dinosaurs.

Hitchcock went back to basics and studied how living animals made tracks. He chased all sorts of critters—chickens, raccoons, frogs, turtles—over muddy fields and diagrammed their tracks. The Reverend soon knew more about the animal sole than any other person. His Jurassic track-makers were way, way different from lizards, crocs, and flat-footed mammals.

giant hip!

megalosaur corrected

Hitchcock's animals walked on their hind legs, not on all fours. They were toe-walkers, which held their ankles high off the ground. Their hind feet had three big toes pointing forward, plus a little one sticking out to the inside. And they had long strides, which meant very long, slender legs. What animal group had legs and feet like that?

BIRDS!

"My Jurassic predators were birds!" Hitchcock wrote in 1838. "The Jurassic and Cretaceous were ruled by an extinct group of ground birds, some as heavy as elephants."

Microraptor

Dilong

Scientists all over the world agreed. But part of the mystery remained. If giant Jurassic and Cretaceous birds had been so common, how come no one could find their skeletons? It was a double puzzle: flat-footed dinos left no tracks, and mega-birds left no bones.

In 1867, the problem was solved. Professor Edward Cope in New Jersey and Professor Thomas Huxley in England independently realized that megalosaur skeletons had been put together all wrong. The "shoulder bone" was really part of the hip. The real front leg was thin, and the hind leg was enormous, with a very long shin and ankle. Assembled correctly, megalosaurs weren't flat-footed. They stood on their three long toes with ankles held high. In other words, they were built like gigantic turkeys!

All those predator tracks from the Jurassic and Cretaceous had been made by dinosaurs—dinosaurs that moved like ground birds.

Confuciusornis

Therizinosaurus

Oviraptor

Microraptor

Enantiornis

Yutyrannus

Microraptor

Velociraptor

Cope and Huxley wondered, if dinosaurs had birdlike bones, did some of them actually evolve into birds? It was a mind-boggling thought because it meant that dinosaurs weren't really extinct. The idea was backed up by a newly discovered fossil—*Archaeopteryx,* a Jurassic carnivore the size of a crow. It had sharp teeth, curved claws, and a long bony tail, like a proper little dinosaur. But its skin, preserved as imprints in the rock, was shocking. On the forearm and wrist were big feathers, exactly like a modern bird's. *Archaeopteryx* was a near-perfect missing link between a normal predatory dinosaur and a modern bird.

Most scientists were convinced: birds evolved from mini-dinos. But did dinosaurs have feathers? No one could be sure.

A century later, in the 1960s, Professor John Ostrom discovered *Deinonychus,* a meat-eating dinosaur as heavy as a wolf. *Deinonychus* and its close relative *Velociraptor* had arms, hips, and legs almost exactly like *Archaeopteryx*'s.

Gigantoraptor

Deinonychus

The question came up again: could meat-eating dinosaurs have been covered with feathers? Fossil skin had been found for many dino species, and it was all covered with flat scales. But these skin specimens came from plant-eaters. Were meat-eaters different? Some young paleontologists (including me) drew *Deinonychus* and its relatives with feathers. It just made sense that such birdlike bodies would have birdlike skin. We needed meat-eater specimens with skin.

Indisputable proof was found in 1995, near the village of Liaoning, China. Paleontologists found hundreds of fossilized birds from the Jurassic and Early Cretaceous in the bottoms of lakes. The bird bodies had been buried in mud that was so black and smelly it kept away the crayfish and worms that usually destroy soft tissue. So the Liaoning sediments preserved not just the skeletons but skin as well. Many Liaoning bird fossils have beautifully preserved feathers.

The meat-eating dinosaurs found in the same layers have preserved skin, too! Some of the Liaoning dinos are close relatives of *Ornitholestes, Velociraptor,* and *Deinonychus.* Others are

Sinosauropteryx

Sinornithosaurus

kin of tyrannosaurs and therizinosaurs (strange dinos with long front claws and stubby tails). Did these meat-eaters have scaly skin? No. All had feathers! Some had wide feathers like those of *Archaeopteryx.* Others had narrow feathers like a kiwi bird's.

If you had a live *T. rex* sitting on your lap right now, what would it feel like? Warm and fluffy.

Caudipteryx

DINOSAURS OF THE SAND DUNES

Feathered dinosaurs spread through all sorts of habitats. If we traveled back to the heart of central Asia in the Late Cretaceous, we'd see some fluffy dinos raising their families in pink sand dunes.

*Oviraptor*s search for fruit and small prey in the bushes around the ponds nestled between the dunes. They're smart—the bones around their brains bulge out because the brains are big. Big brains let *Oviraptor*s learn more quickly than their ancestors where to find food and how to make a nest and how to escape the many new enemies that have now evolved.

*Oviraptor*s have sprinters' legs—long shins and ankles that let them zip away from danger. But when the nest needs protection, *Oviraptor*s must stay and fight. And here comes one of the most deadly enemies, the poison dragon lizard, *Estesia*. *Estesia* has the same weapons as modern Gila monsters. Grooves in its teeth channel poisonous saliva deep into its prey. If an *Oviraptor* was bitten, the poison would cause it to become weak and woozy. In a few minutes, the *Oviraptor* would collapse.

Estesia

Estesia flicks its forked tongue. It smells eggs. The *Oviraptor* mother slashes at the intruder with her long front claws and kicks at it with her powerful hind legs. Meanwhile, the *Oviraptor* father spreads his feathered forelimbs wide like a shield to protect the eggs. The lizard gets away with just one egg.

The Cretaceous sand dunes have left us incredibly beautiful fossils. Massive sandstorms buried thousands of little lizards, small dinosaurs, and furry mammals. The thick sand layer preserved every bone in their skeletons. One father *Oviraptor* got buried as he hunkered down over his nest, trying to keep the sand from smothering the eggs. After the storm, his skeleton was preserved on top of the fossilized eggshells. An expedition from New York City's American Museum of Natural History found the specimens in 1925.

Oviraptor

Zalambdalestes

DINOSAURS IN THE SNOW

Scientists used to think dinosaurs couldn't live in snowy regions. That's because we assumed dinosaurs were like lizards and turtles—animals who can't produce much body heat. A lizard-like dinosaur out in a cold wind would get frostbite and die.

Now we know better. Dinosaurs were built more like hot-blooded birds than cold-blooded reptiles. When you look at dinosaur bone under a microscope, you see it's full of tiny holes for little blood vessels. That means that the blood flow was high and the body generated a lot of heat.

Edmontosaurus

We find Cretaceous dinosaurs in Alaska, but was Alaska cold back then? What we need is a paleo-thermometer—and fossil leaves are just that. Today, plants in warm environments have rounded leaves with down-turned tips that let rainwater drip off. In cold habitats, leaves have zigzaggy edges and no drip tips. Fossil leaves prove that Cretaceous winters in Alaska were snowy. Not as cold as today, but still cold enough to freeze a tortoise solid. Meat-eating dinosaurs could survive the Alaskan winter because they had fluffy feathers to keep warm. Big veggie-saurs might have migrated south.

Imagine we're in Alaska in October about 74 million years ago. Herds of *Pachyrhinosaurus* snort and stomp as they get ready to migrate to southern Canada, six hundred miles away.

Animals have to be big to walk that far. That's because big animals walk more efficiently than little ones. Little dinosaurs must stay in Alaska as winter comes. Perhaps the turkey-sized predator *Troodon* (TRO-uh-don) got new snowy-white feathers for camouflage. In deep snow, the *Troodon*s would be almost invisible, perfect for hunting little mammals shaped like fat chipmunks. There's one now! *Fwump. Crrrunch. Yum.*

Pachyrhinosaurus

Troodon

DINOSAUR ORCHESTRA

When the herds arrive at their winter headquarters in Alberta and Montana, the singing begins. To be a success in evolution, a dinosaur has to find food and defeat its enemies. But that's not enough. A dinosaur has to attract a mate and have healthy baby dinosaurs that grow up and have babies of their own.

Modern-day land animals use all sorts of ways to attract mates. Bull moose waggle their antlers to attract cows. Elk make bugling noises. Many birds jump and dance and make a ruckus. What did dinosaurs do? They sang!

Parasaurolophus

Daspletosaurus

parksosaurs

Flat-headed duckbill dinosaurs had huge holes in their snout bones. In life, the skin of the nostrils covered the holes. When the duckbill snorted, the holes worked like echo chambers to make a super-loud sound. Subdivisions in the echo chamber would produce multiple notes during each snort. Horned dinosaurs also had wide echo chambers built into their muzzles, as did the dinosaur tanks, the ankylosaurians.

Crested duckbills evolved even more complicated instruments. They had hollow bone tubes that connected their throats to their nostrils. Some species had tubes that bent around like a French horn. Other species had tubes arranged like a bassoon. Bones vibrate like hard wood, so when the dinosaur blew air through the tubes, the skull worked like a giant woodwind instrument.

Parasaurolophus

Corythosaurus

Styracosaurus

Euoplocephalus

Each species had its own style of noisemaker. In the spring, the combined calls of a dozen species must have been like a Cretaceous orchestra.

Noisemakers in the skull might solve the mystery of how duckbills defended themselves. Big animals can make sounds that are so loud and deep that the ground shakes. Elephants do that today. And super-loud sounds can be a weapon. When an elephant gives out a blast of earthquake noise, it can make you dizzy and dopey.

Maybe, just maybe, when a herd of duckbills was approached by a tyrannosaur, the veggie-saurs would all turn their heads and snort!

Some dinosaurs probably performed a mating dance. Ostrich dinos had long necks, long arms, and super-long shins and ankles. Birds with that build often leap and bounce in courtship dance steps.

T. rex and other giant meat-eaters couldn't sing well. The echo chambers in their skulls were small. So how did they attract mates? Interesting question . . .

Edmontonia

Euoplocephalus

Ornithomimus

Centrosaurus

Tyrannosaurus

CRETACEOUS ANTI-TANK WEAPON: *TYRANNOSAURUS REX*

The very last big dinosaur predators were the mighty *Tyrannosaurus rex* and its close kin, which grew as heavy as small elephants. Some other carnivores had bodies that were bigger. Some had skulls that were longer. But no other carnivorous dinosaur had jaws or a neck stronger than *T. rex*'s.

Tyrannosaurus rex neck bones were huge and arranged in a big S-curve. Powerful neck muscles could pull the head back and sideways. When a *T. rex* grabbed struggling prey, it could shake its victim senseless. Strong biting muscles in its skull could slam the jaws shut with a mighty chomp.

Sometimes books and movies call *T. rex* a sharp-tooth, but that's wrong. Primitive members of the tyrannosaur family did have sharp tooth crowns—*Nanotyrannus*, which lived with *T. rex,* still had these narrow meat-slicers. But *T. rex* teeth evolved in a new direction. Its crowns were thick and blunt, like bananas. That shape isn't for slicing soft flesh—it's for crushing bones and cracking thick armor.

Tyrannosaurus rex was a self-propelled anti-tank weapon. It needed the upgraded weaponry because it had to deal with better-protected veggie-saur species.

Club-tailed dino-tanks and shoulder-spiked dinosaurs were stronger than they had been ten million years earlier. *Triceratops* was twice as heavy as its earlier relative *Chasmosaurus*.

And *Triceratops* had better protection. Most horned dinosaurs had bony neck shields with holes in the center. Tough skin covered the holes. But T'tops developed neck shields made of solid bone.

In front of its shield, *Triceratops* had very long horns over the eyes—one well-aimed thrust could kill any other dinosaur. *T. rex* needed all its newly evolved armament to fight a *Triceratops* and win.

Triceratops

Euoplocephalus

Occasionally a *T. rex* might find a dead T'tops and get a free meal. But most of the time, *T. rex*es would have to kill their own prey. Live T'topses were always dangerous. A solo duckbill might have been an easy kill, but they traveled in huge herds that would have been hard to attack. Some duckbill skeletons have old tyrannosaur bites on their backbones—wounds that had healed. That means a duckbill could, on occasion, escape a tyrannosaur attack.

Tyrannosaurus rex survived for almost two million years, so on average, it won enough battles to feed itself. And somehow it was a success as a parent. Remember—every dinosaur had to attract a mate, and that includes *T. rex.* How could such a scary predator express romantic feelings? Hand claws give a clue. Primitive tyrannosaurs, like *Nanotyrannus,* had big, hooked claws. *Tyrannosaurus rex* evolved unusual hands—the fingers were weak and the claws were blunt and smaller than *Nanotyrannus*'s even though the *T. rex*'s body was ten times heavier. Professor Henry Fairfield Osborn, whose crew announced the first *T. rex* in 1905, had an outrageous idea: *Tyrannosaurus* was a . . . tickler! Osborn believed that evolution gave *T. rex* delicate fingers so it could give gentle touches. A male *T. rex* would slowly approach a female, then reach out and stroke her.

T. rex

DUEL AT THE END OF DINOSAUR TIME

We're in Wyoming, 66 million years ago, at the end of the Cretaceous. It's hot and humid, like Louisiana today.

Turtles, crocodiles, and alligators build their nests in the sun-warmed sand. Mammals scamper over fallen logs and up into the trees. The biggest furball, *Didelphodon*—nicknamed "the Cretaceous Taz"—cavorts in a stream. It has a head like a Tasmanian devil and the body of an otter. Pterodactyls loom large. *Quetzalcoatlus* and its relatives soar overhead on wings that span over thirty-five feet across. Under the shade of a cypress tree, *T. rex* parents feed their newly hatched chicks.

Quetzalcoatlus

baby rexes

Didelphodon

With a loud hoot, an angry bull *Triceratops* breaks through the cattail rushes and charges at the *T. rex*es. It's mating season and the bull is raging with hormones—chemicals in his bloodstream that make him want to fight everybody everywhere. But Mom and Dad *T. rex* won't leave their babies. They step out to meet the threat. The T'tops turns sharply left and swivels his head. His horn nicks Dad. *Ouch.* Mom snaps her head forward and bites at the T'tops's frill. *Clunk-crunch.* Her teeth nip into the thick bone.

The T'tops swings his head around and bellows. His brow horns penetrate the dad's thigh. The bull backs up a half step to deliver the killing blow. . . . *Whump!* The female *rex* jumps right on top of the T'tops's wide backside and bites at his neck. Both *rex*es and the T'tops roll over, churning up the water. Mud and algae and blood go flying. Finally, the T'tops emerges. He hoots and walks away. The *rex*es hobble out of the stream. Both are hurt. But they'll live.

azhdarchid

Borealosuchus

Triceratops

T. rex

DINOSAUR EXTINCTION AND US

Triceratops and *T. rex* kept feeding, fighting, and reproducing until about 65.5 million years ago. And then they were gone. All the other big dinosaur species died out, too. The only part of the dino family tree that remained was the birds. In the oceans, giant swimming reptiles died out and so did many kinds of shellfish. What happened?

This wasn't the first mega-die-off in the earth's history. Big predators and herbivores had become extinct in the Permian, Triassic, and Jurassic Periods. Every thirty million years or so, disaster had struck land life.

To find out what happened, it helps to look at who survived the extinction. When *T. rex* died out, the freshwater crocodiles, alligators, and big soft-shell turtles kept on going, right to the present day. Salamanders, frogs, lizards, and snakes also did fine. They have more species now than they did in the Cretaceous.

One theory is that furry mammals ate all the dino eggs. But mammals eat gator and turtle eggs today and these reptiles survive. Here's another theory: super-volcanoes blew up, blocking the sun with volcanic ash and making the winters cooler on land. Problem is, tropical turtles, crocs, and gators need warm, wet conditions and they survived.

Borealosuchus

Protungulatum

The most popular theory says that a meteorite smashed into the earth, sending up a dust cloud that cooled the land and polluted the water with acid rain. But this theory has holes, too. Warmth-loving crocs, gators, and turtles didn't die out. Plus frogs and salamanders survived, even though acid rain kills most amphibians.

An old theory says that dinosaurs traveled from one continent to another, spreading diseases. I like this idea. Big land animals travel faster than little ones, and faster than river reptiles like crocs and gators. So big dinosaurs could spread diseases faster and farther than little lizards on land and big reptiles in rivers and lakes.

Maybe we need to combine several theories?

The biggest surprise is that one group of animals "enjoyed" the dinosaur extinction—our very own warm-blooded mammalian class! Remember—we mammals first evolved way back in the Triassic, the time of the earliest dinosaurs. While dinosaurs got bigger and bigger, mammals stayed small. Meat-eating dinosaurs chased us from the Triassic right through the Cretaceous.

So how did we mammals survive? By scampering away into burrows and hollow trees. We had to stay small so we could hide.

As long as dinosaurs ruled the land, our mammal ancestors couldn't evolve to become big. But when the dinos disappeared, mammal evolution was unleashed. Some mammals became hoofed animals, like horses, rhinos, hippos, antelope, deer, and giraffes. Others evolved into meat-eaters, like wolves, bears, hyenas, and tigers. Still others became specialized bug-eaters, like anteaters and armadillos.

brachiosaurs

fish

first reptiles

early dinosaur

tyrannosaur

first amphibians

fin-backs

duckbills

horned dinos

raptors

proto-mammal

first mammals

primates

frogs

There was one little furball survivor that evolved in a very special way. At first it didn't look like much—just a fuzzy, hedgehog-like beast that chased beetles and licked nectar from flowers. But soon after the big dinos died, it became a sharp-eyed tree-climber with nails on its fingertips instead of claws. It could scamper up trees and bushes, holding on to slender branches.

That little fellow was the earliest primate.

lizards

crocodiles

birds

humans

apes

cetaceans

By the end of the Cretaceous, most early mammals were brainier than lizards, snakes, and frogs. Early primates, however, evolved bigger brains even faster than did most other mammals. Fifty-five million years ago, some primates became tarsier-like creatures that leaped across the treetops. Forty million years ago, some of these leapers became apes.

Seven million years ago, an ape evolved into a hominid with hind legs built for walking upright. Now its arms could be used for carrying food or holding babies. Or chipping rocks to make tools.

Fifty thousand years ago, one hominid species became so clever that it started making sewing needles from bones, and sharp little knives for cutting shirts and trousers from animal skins. These hominids began making sculptures and paintings on the walls of caves. They had become the species called *Homo sapiens*. They were *us*!

And while the big dinosaurs are long gone, one clan still lives. The birds! Almost ten thousand species of birds are alive today, so we have more species of dinosaurs now than in the Jurassic or Cretaceous!

Dinosaurs are with us in another way, too. By chasing our ancestors for so many millions of years, dinosaurs sent us down evolutionary paths toward quicker feet and more nimble brains. When those big dinosaurs finally died out, we were ready to take their place in nature.

So the dinosaur story is really our story, too.

INDEX AND GUIDE TO PRONUNCIATION

Map showing where Cretaceous Period dinosaurs
and other famous fossils are dug today